BLAZERS

Wild Outdoors

Ice Fishing

by Jeanie Mebane

Reading Consultant: Barbara J. Fox
Reading Specialist
North Carolina State University

CAPSTONE PRESS
a capstone imprint

Blazers is published by Capstone Press,
151 Good Counsel Drive, P.O. Box 669, Mankato, Minnesota 56002.
www.capstonepub.com

Books published by Capstone Press are manufactured with paper
containing at least 10 percent post-consumer waste.

Library of Congress Cataloging-in-Publication Data
Mebane, Jeanie.
Ice fishing / by Jeanie Mebane.
    p. cm. — (Blazers. Wild outdoors)
  Includes bibliographical references and index.
  Summary: "Describes the equipment, skills, and techniques needed for ice fishing"—Provided
by publisher.
  ISBN 978-1-4296-6006-8 (library binding)
 1. Ice fishing—Juvenile literature. I. Title. II. Series.
  SH455.45.M43 2012
  799.12'2—dc22   2011003783

Editorial Credits

Angie Kaelberer, editor; Gene Bentdahl and Bobbie Nuytten, designers; Sarah Schuette,
    photo stylist; Marcy Morin, scheduler; Eric Manske, production specialist

Photo Credits

AP Images: Havre Daily News/Nikki Carlson, 9; Capstone Studio: Karon Dubke, 4¬–5, 6 (left),
10, 13, 14–15, 16–17, 18–19 (all), 21, 24, 25, 26–27; iStockphoto: Marcel Pelletier, 20, Michael
Olson, 22 (left); Newscom: MCT/Bruce Bisping, 28–29; Shutterstock: Anteromite, 12, Maxim
Petrichuk, 23, Peter1977, 6–7, Stephen Mcsweeny, cover

Artistic Effects

Capstone Studio: Karon Dubke (woods); Shutterstock: rvika (wood), rvrspb (fence),
VikaSuh (sign)

Printed in the United States of America Stevens Point, Wisconsin.
032011   006111WZF11

Table of Contents

Chapter 1

On the Ice

You lower your fishing line through a hole in the ice on a frozen lake. Sips of hot cocoa help you stay warm in the ice house.

Wild Fact:

Most U.S. ice fishing takes place in northern states. But people also ice fish on mountain lakes as far south as New Mexico and Arizona.

A hungry fish takes your **bait**. You crank your **reel** to pull up the fish through the hole. You just caught a 6-pound (2.7-kilogram) northern pike!

bait—small fish, worms, insects, or other food used to attract fish

reel—a spool or wheel that holds fishing line

Fish are less active in winter, but they still search for food.

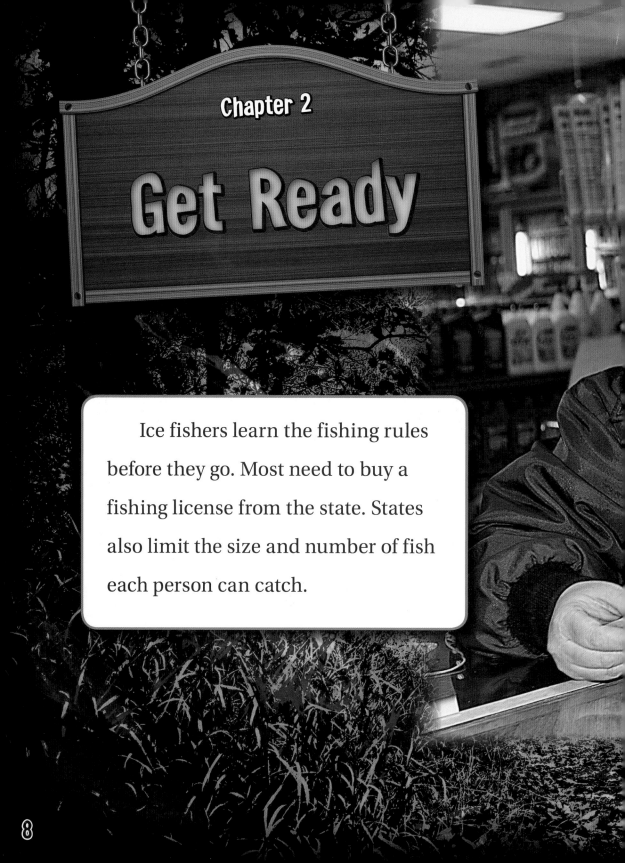

Chapter 2

Get Ready

Ice fishers learn the fishing rules before they go. Most need to buy a fishing license from the state. States also limit the size and number of fish each person can catch.

Wild Fact:

The age that a person needs to begin buying a fishing license varies by state.

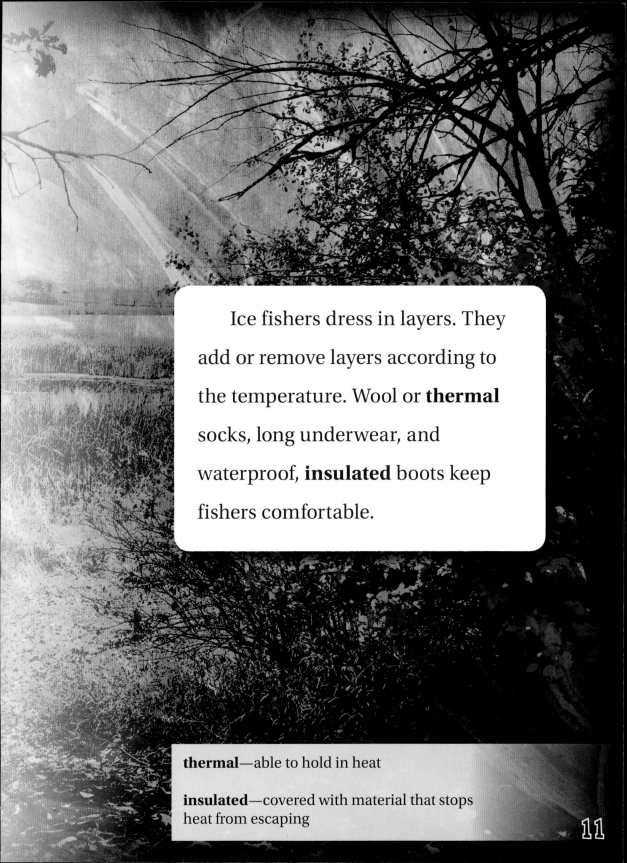

Ice fishers dress in layers. They add or remove layers according to the temperature. Wool or **thermal** socks, long underwear, and waterproof, **insulated** boots keep fishers comfortable.

thermal—able to hold in heat

insulated—covered with material that stops heat from escaping

11

Ice fishers use **chisels** or ice **augers** to make holes in the ice. Some augers are operated by hand. Others are powered by gas or electricity.

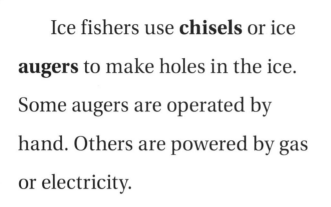

Wild Fact:

Ice fishing rods are short. Fishers hold them over the hole or fasten them into a holder beside the hole.

chisel—a tool with a sharp cutting edge on a strong blade

auger— a sharp tool that uses a screw mechanism to drill holes

Fishers attach bait or **lures** to their fishing lines. Lures look, move, and sometimes even sound or smell like fish **prey**.

lure—an object tied to the end of a fishing line to attract fish

prey—an animal eaten by another animal for food

Ice Fishing Equipment

ice house

heater

contour maps

propane tank

fish finder

fishing license

16

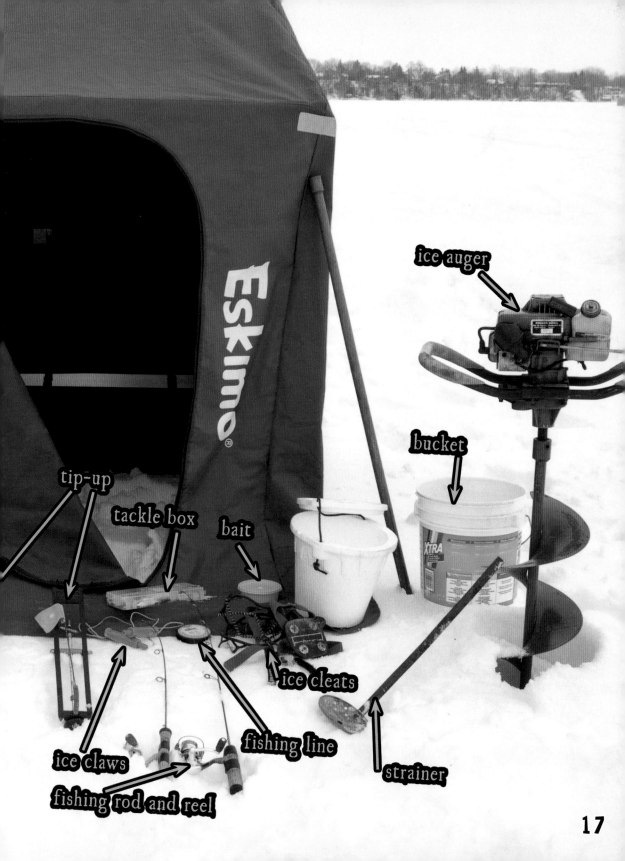

ice auger

bucket

tip-up

tackle box

bait

ice cleats

ice claws

fishing line

fishing rod and reel

strainer

17

Chapter 3

Skills and Techniques

Ice fishers drill holes through the ice and remove slush. They drop their lines into the holes. When the **sinkers** hit bottom, fishers pull the lines up 1 to 2 feet (0.3 to 0.6 meter).

sinker—a weight for sinking fishing line below the surface of the water

Fishers **jig** their lines to attract fish. They watch their **tip-ups**. Tip-up flags flip when fish bite. Then fishers lightly jerk their lines to set the hooks.

jig—to move up and down or side to side

tip-up—a device that holds fishing line and raises a flag when fish bite

Some reels have bells or rattles that make noise when a fish bites.

tip-up

Chapter 4

Safety

No ice is completely safe. Clear ice needs to be at least 4 inches (10 centimeters) thick to safely walk on it. Slushy, snowy ice must be twice as thick as clear ice to be safe for ice fishing.

Wild Fact:

Workers at bait shops and resorts can be good sources of information on ice thickness.

Some equipment helps keep ice fishers safe. **Cleats** help fishers avoid slipping on the ice. **Ice claws** worn around their necks help them escape if they fall through the ice.

cleats

cleats—strips with sharp points that are attached to the sole of a boot to provide traction

ice claws—a short rope with sharp spikes attached to handles at each end

ice claw

Wild Fact:

Ice claw spikes grip the ice, allowing fishers to pull their bodies from the water.

25

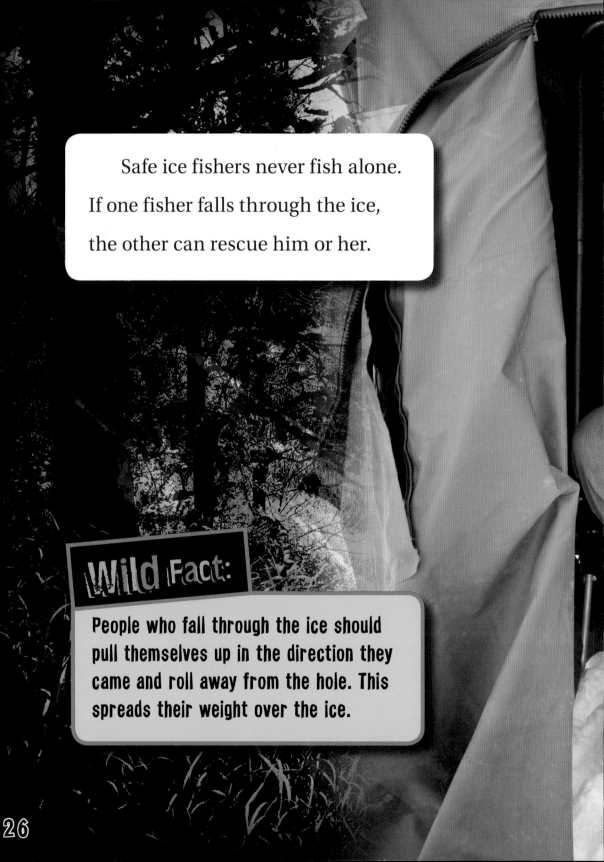

Safe ice fishers never fish alone. If one fisher falls through the ice, the other can rescue him or her.

Wild Fact:

People who fall through the ice should pull themselves up in the direction they came and roll away from the hole. This spreads their weight over the ice.

Chapter 5

Ice-Cold Fun

You and a friend drill holes in the ice and set your tip-ups. Suddenly two flags flip up. You both have fish to fry for dinner!

Wild Fact:

Many ice fishers compete in tournaments. Each year more than 11,000 fishers take part in the Ice Fishing Extravaganza near Brainerd, Minnesota.

Glossary

auger (AW-guhr)—a sharp tool that uses a screw mechanism to drill holes

bait (BAYT)—tiny fish or other food used to attract fish

chisel (CHIZ-uhl)—a tool with a sharp cutting edge on a strong blade

cleats (KLEETZ—strips with sharp points attached to the sole of a boot to provide traction on ice

ice claws (EYESS KLAWZ)—a short rope with sharp spikes attached to handles at each end

insulated (in-suh-LAY-tuhd)—covered with material that stops heat from escaping

jig (JIG)—to move up and down or side to side

lure (LOOR)—an object designed to attract fish

reel (REEL)—a spool or wheel that holds fishing line; reels are attached to fishing rods and turned by a hand crank

prey (PRAY)—an animal eaten by another animal for food

sinker (SING-ker)—a weight that sinks the fishing line below the surface of the water

thermal (THUR-muhl)—able to hold in heat

tip-up (tip-UP)—a device that raises a flag when a fish bites

Read More

DiLorenzo, Michael. *Adventures with Jonny: Ice Fishing.* Clinton Township, Mich.: Running Moose Publications, 2007.

Dyer, Hadley, and Bobbie Kalman. *Fishing in Action.* Sports in Action. New York: Crabtree Pub., 2006.

Salas, Laura Purdie. *Ice Fishing.* The Great Outdoors. Mankato, Minn.: Capstone Press, 2008.

Internet Sites

FactHound offers a safe, fun way to find Internet sites related to this book. All of the sites on FactHound have been researched by our staff.

Here's all you do:

Visit *www.facthound.com*

Type in this code: 9781429660068

Index